M000087727

Nature Lovers

books by

Charles Potts

Nature Lovers

Charles Potts

Pleasure Boat Studio

Copyright © 2000 by Charles Potts

All rights reserved.

ISBN: 1-929355-04-1

Library of Congress Card Number: 00-102214

Pleasure Boat Studio
8630 NE Wardwell Road
Bainbridge Island, WA 98110

Tel-Fax 1-888-810-5308
Email: pleasboat@aol.com
URL: http://www.pbstudio.com

Cover design: "Nature Lovers" plus section breaks
by Robert McNealy

Printed in the United States of America by Thomson-Shore

First Edition

Acknowledgments:

Some of the poems in *Nature Lovers* were previously
published in the following magazines and anthologies.
Thanks are due to Stephen Jacobsen of Guerrilla Poetics
Press and *Rhododendron* in Salt Lake City and Palo Alto;
Penelope Reedy and *The Redneck Review of Literature* in
Twin Falls, Idaho, and Milwaukee, Wisconsin; James
Mechem of *Caprice* in Wichita, Kansas; *Maverick Western
Verse* from Gibbs Smith, publisher, Layton, Utah, and *The
Dry Crik Review*, both edited by John C. Dofflemyer of
Lemon Cove, California; Rick Ardinger of *Boise Magazine*,
Boise, Idaho; Bret Axel of *Will Work For Peace* from
Zeropanik Press, Trenton, New Jersey; and Steve Durland
of *High Performance*, Los Angeles, California.

Nature Lovers

Overamping in Walla Walla

The Henry David Thoreau Volunteer Army

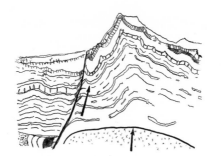

Nature Lovers

Nature Lovers

Nature lovers unite!
We have only to defeat the fear
Of the dirty little secret
At the heart of the dark:
Everybody's somebody else's lunch.

It's been a weird gig
To be the broken link
In the food chain of fools,
Masticating our way to the elusive apex,
At the pinnacle of arrogance on the food pyramid.

Nobody eats this meat, we insist:
Neither bear nor beast
Nor breast of mama
Deprives the worms as well in death,
Consumed entirely by flames.

For far too long we conceived in nature
As a pastoral binge
Out of some off the wall city escape
To a babbling brook with a babbling broad
Away from the millions we considered highly unnatural.

The billions crawl and mall and trade
Their commercial appetites in
For something insatiable to the last bite.
Nature has the last laugh —
Compost full of grace.

The State of Nature

*You are obfuscating me, but I say, that I never
joined the union never left the union never
re-entered the union never accepted the
hospitality never was an independent state
never has ceased being as a separate nation.*

Charles Foster
Peyote Toad

I am living proof of the Platonic Principle
That poets should not be permitted in *The Republic*.
Republicans, who confuse their fly fishing trips
With the evil art of destroying the environment while
Pretending to protect it, should not be permitted in nature.

Plato, unable to conceive of zero,
Zeroed out the Dionysians
In favor of logic of all things
And did his indelible bit to create
The Department of Mental Illness.

There may still be a little nature left in every state.
I've never been to Alabama.
Let's elevate the state of our own nature
To a perspective worth reviewing the spectacle from.
Will you join me in a voyage of discovery?
Can you help kick over the traces?

The Stream of Consciousness

The stream of consciousness flows
Effortlessly forward like an unfed brain,
Given nothing new to think about,
Merely rotates in space, the same sounds,
Pictures, and sensations in predictable order.

Who will muddy up this stream,
Then purge and purify the cluttered tableau
Of the extraneous features preventing you
From actualizing your ideal self,
The way you always wanted to look and sound?

The quicksand of the collective unconsciousness
Will tempt you many times
With its lurid renditions of quackery images
Stored in the millennia of Christian denial,
Hallucinated forward at the speed of pain.

Down a lazy river to the polluted sea
The flotsam jettisons thoughtlessly along,
Contributory to a natural disaster.
Throw yourself onto the banks to stimulate
Your freeflowing sense of contrary motion.

The Code of the Olde West
(Violations of Natural Law)

Get a load of Charlie Coyote,
Hauled before the magistrate by the grammar police
For hunting verbs without a license.

The judge demands to know:
How did you learn the vernacular?
There are correct ways to say the same thing.

Cheap talk from fatigued Sierra Clubbers
Cannot change my mind, your honor.
I'm outside the purview of Standard American Englishizers.

Like the taxidermist he will be
If he ever catches anything Stoic,
Stuff this poem and make it snappy naturally.
Fill it with linguistic drift.

The Cutting Edge

We surf through life on the cutting curl,
The ultimate edge of enlightenment,
Waiting for our new associates to
Disambiguate the next second.

We can do it ourselves, you know.
The most mysterious quality of the next second is
That it hasn't happened yet.

Hoist anchor.
Predict the future, re-write the past.
Check your armor at the door.
Open up the future with feeling.

Watch where you're going.

The Chinese solution to this is to imagine
Time going up in the morning
And down in the afternoon.

Time like the tail of an unchartered comet
Streams out behind us like the fossil record.
History is time condensed in space.

I wanna be at the head of the comet,
Light bent back around my ears.
Time is warped.
I'd rather be surfing through space.

Natural High

"I do not take drugs, I am drugs,"
Salvador Dali is supposed to have sneered.

"History is a fable agreed upon,"
Napoleon retorted.

"Take the risks of interpreting the meeting
Of natural history and cultural history,"
Carl Ortwin Sauer admonished his acolytes.

Take a flying leap at a spatial construct
Built like a bird from twigs still lying
Or otherwise found around the house.

Three wise men cannot singly fathom
My collective use of their coin of our realm.
Our house is in place and refuses to budge.

My brain contains every way I ever wanted to feel.
Staying in one place makes attempting to duck
Responsibilities no longer an option.

Down the brain drain with a human plant,
Peyote once placed me with my eyes and ears
Geosynchronous with the troubled horizon.

More about that later when I come up for air.
For now be high in a natural stretch.
Think yourself taller and your body will trunkify.

With nowhere to go we can only improve
The depth of our meticulous appreciation
For the green and growing rizosphere we call home.
We are all turning into Douglas Firs.

Donner Beach Party

Far into the background of *Moby Dick*,
A whaling ship in the South Pacific
Was rammed by a sperm whale,
And the survivors set out in whaling boats
To eat each other toward South America.

When the Moslems arrived in Europe
With the zero they'd kiped from the Hindus
They were thanked for delivering nothing
And told at Tours in very certain terms
To get and stay the hell out of there.

We are still at the level of the Bertillon* process
For identifying the individual characteristics of criminals:
How wide is the forehead? How long is the forearm?
How crooked is the length of the knucklewalker's penis?
Where do we go from here?

So like a cannibal to start hoarding biscuits.
Beirut is a city of the future where everybody's a terrorist.
Cannibalism, counting, and criminality,
Could all be banned from the natural world.
RSVP, you're invited to the party.

*Alphonse Bertillon, 19th Century French anthropologist

Natural Causes

"He died of natural causes."
How many times have you relaxed while reading
That sanguine phrase and paused to wonder:
What causes would not be natural?

Car wrecks, overdoses, the fall of flight DC 10?
Mechanical, pharmaceutical, aeronautical?
If everything is by definition natural,
What's left to experiment on?

Pig out on Haagen Daz ice cream diet?
Fall down my one-time publisher's nomenclature,
The Empty Elevator Shaft?
Will you pass on in a drug bust or a cardiac arrest?

You ask too many questions.
See death of a naturalist.
Watch Hermes put Argus to sleep
With an interminable story.
Bored him to death, naturally.

The Meaning of "Good Natured"

We used to share the planet
With millions of other creatures and species,
But one by one we've eaten, exploited, and
Otherwise destroyed virtually everything
We could get our manipulatable hands on.

Condors survive in condor coops,
Pandas on the last few dozen bamboo shoots,
Whales on Nippon scientific whaling,
Grizzlies in an undeveloped country called Canada,
Elephants on the free trade Hong Kong road to death.

There must be some good news in here someplace.
Beyond cockroaches, coyotes and the genetic decoding
Scavengers of our excess, lies the microbiologic
Success stories within our own cancer ridden
Pesticidal, herbicidal, insecticidal bodies.

When suicidal success is a virus thriving
On any bit of reduplicatable cell matter,
Eating their host as they go on
Bingeing with double talk when success is failure,
When is God going to sober us up?

Natural Language

I've had other friends who've studied Chinese
And became even more serious and specific
About each kind of tree,
Bird beast and flower and the names of things.

For me, it satisfies my earth bound nature,
Stimulates me to soar through the fathomless middle,
Where what's real is not things and feet set in concrete
But impulses, particles, and waves.

Give me your liptons, your muons,
Your quarks, yearning to be free.

I've said all I can about the places I've been.
I've told the truth and the truth hurts and frees.
I'm feeling the oats of a second childhood.
Be prepared to believe you ain't seen nothing yet.

We're coming out of the clouds on a terminal wave
Of dysfunctional rectilinear logic.
Which might mean we've had our heads up our asses
To think we can get away with all the shit we've pulled.

You are what you eat; where you shit is our business.
You will be tied to your wastes and leftovers,
Nuclear and otherwise, by the specific gravity of our situation.
How does it feel to have six billion people in your family?

English is the language of freedom.
American English even moreso.
The freedom to abstract responsibilities
And palm them off on unprepared defendants.

The Rest of the Reformation
For Martin Luther, not King Jr.

Half of all the problems currently bedeviling our planet
Can be traced directly to the bogus belief system
Of the Roman Catholic Church and its distinctly fallible Pope.

Hand in glove with American Confederates,
As close as a condom fits a rigid dick,
Birth control information and abortions are denied
To billions who'd be better of with them.
Population pressure produces pollution,
Reinforcing the ever expanding world economy.

The right to die is denied
To the brain dead, the living dead,
And 10,000 vegetating comatose cases.

This reformation is not about
Turning you into a latter-day Lutheran.
Get rid of the whole fantastic Christian mess.

Take an out to lunch Catholic or Christian out to lunch.
Ask them to get their beliefs out of politics.
Encourage them to think and read.
Thank God the Italians who live closest at hand
Refuse to suffer their stupidities.

The Vatican, Notre Dame, and other Gothic examples
Of demonic architecture
Like the churches that raped Mexico
Will make adequate museums.

From the We're Finally Getting Someplace Department

I always knew Chicago had
The potential to be a leader.

The Catholic Church is closing
25 churches in the Chicago diocese
Due to lack of interest, i.e.,
Money and support.

The lapsed Catholics of Chicago
Go with God's blessing.

May the closings spread like
Fire gone wild
Right up to and including
The dour door of the Vatican.

The Scourge of Environmentalism
or
The Crime of Positive Thinking

The scourge of environ "mentalism" occurs
When you think so much about your environs
That you are incapacitated to do anything about it.

Uninterrupted positive thinking about our problems
Permits us to imagine that
Somebody else is taking care of them.

Which is worse? To act without thinking —
Which got us into this mess?
Or to think without acting —
Which won't get us out of it either?

All the brain power on wobbling earth
Won't psychokineticize a thing.
Does this mean we have to go back to work?

Natural Responsibilities

You get the kind of world
You think it is.

Change your mind.
Change the world.

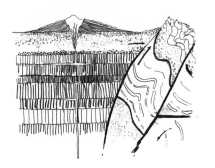

Overamping in Walla Walla

Overamping in Walla Walla

I've been in Walla Walla going on fifteen years,
Doing field study of White Republicans.

To blend in, I joined the Elks Club,
The Benevolent and Protective Order of Same,
And the National Rifle Association.
I ran for city council.
I have a permit to carry a concealed weapon,
Sometimes confused with a license to carry a gun.

110 ten years ago Walla Walla was bigger than Seattle.
We have a steady state economy
That would have warmed the remaining cockles
Of MoDahl's (Morris Udahl's) heart,
Plus a stable population.

If these White Republicans can't solve their own problems,
Then the jig is up.

I resigned from the Elks in disagreement
With their adhoc racism.
My membership in the NRA lapsed.
I lost the election by 146 votes,
But I kept my permit.

The Spotted Owl of Athens

In the old growth forests
Of the Pacific Northwest
It's not only owls we're saving
But our own unregenerate souls.

Let a huge outcry resound
At the capitol in Olympia.

It's no accident that the owl is the Goddess
Athena's great speckled bird of wisdom.

Nor that Athena should have sprung full grown
Out of her father Zeus's head,
Who was trying to swallow and deny the truth.

Like a Doug Fir or a cosmic erection,
You can't keep a good idea down.

Miracle on Main Street

St. George and the Dragon...
Just when you thought we were
Fresh out of dragons,
St. George has found another way to slay us.

Take the Nixon Doctrine of Benign Neglect
To its logical extreme:

Let the blind see,
With a thousand points of light.
Quadriplegics will rise
From their wheel chairs and walk.
Make the angry laugh out loud.

Hitherto hopeless welfare cases
Seek steady employment in the land of plenty.
Stimulate a veteran to pony up
For his own medical expenses.

Federal Funds for Obscene Art

For Senator Jesse Helms,
Republican of North Carolina

More than 1,000 people a day die
In the United States alone,
Killed with tobacco smoke.

Mapplethorpe's photographs haven't killed anybody.
Let's bring the drug war home to roost.
One man's obscenity is the addiction of 100 million.

Is tobacco art? Is tobacco death?
Why should the government fund this farce?
This poem is killing me but I'm a volunteer.

I've created my share of obscene art,
But this isn't some of it.
Find the obscenity in this picture.

I'll forego any further claim to federal funding
When you give up the federal tobacco subsidies
For 30,000 North Carolinian merchants of death.

No Man's Land

for Ray Obermayr

Ray used to wonder out loud
Whether or not I was the first Hippy
Or the last Beatnik.
I never quite fit in either batch —
A man without a movement.

I'm a war baby not a boomer.
I hate this feeling of falling
Between two half-baked cracks.

How can you hope to be avant garde
On a spherical world?
No matter which way you face,
Somebody is always in front of you.

I Play a Lot of Tennis

Loving the game,
I play a lot of tennis
Where you have to be completely ruthless
And absolutely congenial
Simultaneously.

I think it helps me stay in tune
For the bigger matches
With taxes and death.

Lesser Seattle

for Charles Royer
Hizzoner the Mayor (1986-1990)

Seattle is a beautiful city,
But not big enough for its own garbage.

It would rather ship the shit out
To Yakima or Arlington
Than face it down on Fifth Avenue,
Or heaven forbid in the filthy rich
Homes around the arboretum.

The east side of the mountains is not your toilet.
We already have the nation's radioactive
Dog do to deal with.

Find room for your garbage closer to home.
Stack it on a vacant lot
Next door to the seventy floor Columbia Tower.
We've taken all of it we can eat.

The Paul Bunyan Memorial Clearcut

They built the banks that ate Seattle
With proceeds from
The Paul Bunyan Memorial Clearcut.

Columbia Center, First Interstate,
Pacific First, Washington Mutual,
Gateway Towers, Union Square One,
Union Square Two.

Nomenclature chiseled onto glass and granite,
Designed to fool our dreams of steel,
Into thinking we've all been skyscrapered under
This evergreen debt together.

Walk a Mall in My Shoes

(an economic sonnet; sing if you know the tune)

I hear the geriatric types are traipsing
Past Sears and B. Daltons in their Reeboks,
While the poor young men and women workers
Have their FICA raised to underwrite this retirement binge.

Just walk on by; don't buy a thing.
Voluntary economic minimalism
Could cut the gross national product in half.
Save some of the planet for the children.

Act helpless and exercise the right to whine.
It used to get people falling over backwards to help.
Nature disguised as death retired Claude Pepper.
Economic weather report: High pressure — No relief.

If you have the time to walk the malls,
We're going to find you a better job.

The Dexter Manley Solution

The drug problem in Empire America
Boils down to the fact that
Some people who use some drugs
Harass other people who use other drugs.

If we didn't pay professional athletes so much,
They wouldn't be able to afford cocaine.

All the football players who take coke
Could go offshore and form a new team,
The professional cokehead team.

The threat to the NFL will be:
We can beat any team you can field.

Environmental Impact Statement

Would it do
The do-gooders
Any good to know
That people in concentrations
Of more than a few hundred
Are an environmental disaster.

Could this be why I still care more
For the barren reaches of Big Lost River
On horseback far from the Sierra Clubbed
Pavements of the San Francisco Bay?

If agriculture is the original sin
That allowed us to eat well and grow numerous,
What keeps the cure only a cataclysm away?

Wendell Berry behind his horse drawn plow
Is another fly in the amber of the marketplace
Doing the incremental two-step with billions
On our supposed way out of this mess.

Coyotes, cockroaches,
Norwegian wharf rats, viruses,
All star in "The Revenge of the Scavengers."

Who else belongs on the short list of
The species that will be worse off
When human beings suddenly evaporate
From the face of the earth?

A Monkey in the High 90s

Faced with a barrage of excited chattering,
I want so hard to believe there is
A breakthrough just around the corner,
Even though I realize *The Hundredth Monkey*
In the nuclear charade was Comrade Korbachev.

Among the more than 100 suggested ways we could help
To save the planet in the recent *Utne Reader*,
Across the facing page from Christian Ecology are,
"Organize potluck dinners" and
"Be creative with leftovers."

Why not a leftover potluck?
Or better still
A potluck fast:
Just bring your hunger and contemplate.

The Call of Nature

Everywhere the ceremony of innocence is drowned.
William Butler Yeats

The call of nature is a euphemism
For a bowel movement.
Number one or number two?
We were asked as children.

We've sought to be away from
Our bowel movements and their bacterial swarm.

Consider the airborne pollutants from Boise Cascade's
Container division at Wallula Gap,
About which their own scientists say with a straight face:
We don't know what effect they're having,
But we wouldn't dream of endangering anybody's health.

The shitmobile of North America
Was once relatively fresh and
Filled with baffled natives.
Even stale it's still attracting individuals who are
Desperately seeking to avoid their responsibilities
Wherever they started from.

It's not that we don't have "room" for other people.
We don't have room for responsibility avoidance.
If this is the escape hatch for everybody trying to
Avoid the market for panic breeding,
Then when will it get to be such a burden
That Mexico nukes the Vatican to get the point across?

I love a good harangue.
It is said that sometimes you have to write a poem
Just to get the shit out of your mouth.

The Naming of the Age

Civilization is the exact distance between man and his excrement.

Children are named when they are born,
But ages acquire monikers with age,
After their characteristics have been exposed.

The Age of Reason, The Enlightenment,
The Pacific Century, for example.
The last one perhaps a bit premature.

Our own times have been referred to as:
The Atomic Age, the Nuclear Age, the Space Age,
The Age of Aquarius. But none of them stuck.

The Information Age is popular with people
Programmed on Alvin Toffler's wave theory
Who think "information explosion" describes
The accumulated data many still prefer to duck.

It is fitting since we are aging wrapped up
In pollution, waste management, garbage, and sewage,
To christen our age with a proper name.

This is the Age of Excrement.

Flash in the Pan

Not a gold nugget but a glimpse of fate,
Time checked out of and ran amock around
By someone seized with a raunchy impulse
To stimulate the sober into joyful mayhem.

Mayday, live it up, let it lie,
Take me along on the timeless travel.

All work and no play gives Jack a tax problem.
To spend or save, that is out of the question.

Don't panic, we've got loads of time.
We'll probably all die laughing.

The Teflon Poet

Mid-tech by-product of the space race
Bounces ideas back to you
To keep them sticking where they must,
A less than holy communion,
With a gallium arsenide wafer.

As we approach absolute Brahman —
Illimitable, immaterial, and timeless —
Our ethereal baggage is weightless as well.

This is a search of the data base
Of human and non-human intelligence,
A chance for everybody to chime in,
The complete unearthly songs of Pan.

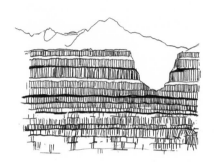

The Henry David Thoreau Volunteer Army

The Henry David Thoreau Volunteer Army

We're looking for a few desperate men
And women, quietness, no problem,
Willing to work long hours
With only intrinsic rewards.

The law abiding can apply elsewhere.
Must be willing to risk jail, poverty,
Death, and the vilification of the state.

Enlist anywhere.
Apply everywhere.
Goto.

Thus Spake Velikovsky

As the apocalypse dawns upon us
One dreary day after another,
I long for the accelerating tables of
Worlds in Collision

Maybe if we could take a hit
From some planetoid the size of Greenland,
Enough dust would be stirred up
To get the climate change off the dime.

With our luck it would probably land
In the ocean somewhere and merely flood
A few dozen self important cities
With some of their own untreated sewage.

Cheap Aristotelian armchair terrorism
Is no suitable substitute
For discovering a mammoth caked in ice,
Its mouth still full of tropical flowers.

Leon Trotsky's Dues Are Refused by the Cascade Chapter of the Washington Sierra Club

Not enough ax murders to go around?
Mexican tourist card expired?

The xylem in your wooden heart
By which our trees and principles stand
Won't hold water.

You scratch your back,
We'll scratch ours.

Retrofit the round the clock revolution.
The truth can never be mashed into shape
Small enough to fit the miserable agenda.

Hyman's Hymn

or

Gassing Up at the Free Market

Barry Hyman suggested that,
"Maybe if you attached a hose to the exhaust pipe
And ran it into the driver's compartment so
No one but the driver would have to breathe it,
Then it would be a free market."

He's a respectable engineer
From the University of Washington,
So he should know:
The full social cost of every item
Has to be built into the price.

Can we start with the BMWs?

My Hat Is in the Ring

(The love song/campaign pledge of
General George Armstrong Custer)

Giddy up Olde Painte,
I'm a leaving Chian.

Where the Buffalo crows
And the crowd jeers
When Lancelot drops his drawers.

It's too far to sense
Two wrong turns to the right,
Now I'll never carry the South
Buried in light.

Buffalo Chips

The Great Plains Computing Company
Is proud to announce the introduction
Of a chip faster than shit,
Where everybody knows the answer
But nobody knows how they got it.

Information disappears so you can dispense with
Lightning-like information storage and retrieval.

Use it and lose it,
Our minds and our memories,
Each moment of asymmetrical time,
Disambiguates the rear view of eternity.

As long as the water's green
And the grass mows endlessly
Where you can see the seas rising
Over Little Bighorn, Montana.

Bionic Raga

I love people but I hate the public.
Deborah Du Nann-Winter, Ph.D.

Mother Teresa saved orphans in an
Overpopulated world.
The hedonist *Bhagwan* Shree Rajneesh
Condemned her from the backseat of
One of 93 Rolls Royces.

The hot wind from the Orient
Blows hard in both directions.
Bhagwan is a Hindu word for God.
Bhagwan is dead; beware of God.

Without good luck but *with* the Catholic Church
We're doing the corporate creep into hyperspace.
You'll have to live inside on Greenhouse Earth,
Or venture out in respirative clothing
Like a deepspace diver in a Neptune storm.
Otherwise the chemicals in our reformed atmosphere
Will eat your flesh before you get
Fifty yards from the house.

We can't all go to outer space
But we can bring it down to earth.

Abandon Hope, Especially Bob

Abandon hope, all ye who comprehend me.
This is not an invitation to the gates of hell.
It's a challenge to imagine the future.

Hope is a debilitating pastime.
When you hope, your internal imagizing capacity
Is coerced into maintaining two
Contradictory visions of the future.

You might think it would only
Reduce your effectiveness by half,
But the grim truth is when you rely on hope
You dissipate all your power to others
Who may not care as much as you do,
Much less about the same things.

Better to imagine you will succeed
And commit yourself to that success.

Never have a nightmare
You can't get lucid in.

The Hothouse Effect

(Formerly the Greenhouse Effect:
a planet full of hot air)

We can barely recall much less return to
A time when the weather went on unabated.

Our ceaseless quest for a 68 degree
Planet at room temperature
Has opened the door to nowhere.

We rely on a room full of scientists, at 98.6,
Who even when they can say for sure
Whether the temperature is going to go up or down,
Will be contradicted by each other and the funny papers
That pass for news and cannot find or stand the truth.

We embrace the averages,
Preferring to avoid the beauty of extremes
Such as the 300 mile an hour winds of Hurricane Pluto
When the bottom drops out of the barometer and everything.

Make Way for Daniel Boone

Is there anybody left unaware
That the planet has been poisoned,
Polluted, and permanently desecrated
By the rapacious hands of man?

My *Greenpeace* magazine flatly states
That half the heavy rock bands
Sold five million albums in the Soviet Union,
While I carry this message with the
High tech equivalent of a pushbroom
Through the potholed streets of Walla Walla.

Give me a break, Daniel Boone. I need
Elbow room from the rock and roll ecologists.
Imagine feeling crowded when the nearest other person
Is twelve miles away!

Put me on the front porch
Of his final frontier cabin,
Jackson County, Missouri, 1803,
Some place to sulk as Lewis and Clark
Bypass my heart on their way west.

The Wooden Heart of John Brown

When Earthfirsters! Get AK-47s
The criminal courtrooms of the American federal system
Will be no place to split the hairs on a ruling
That it's ok to destroy the place
As long as contracts are honored,
Jobs are saved,
And the revenue keeps on rolling in.

When is the civil war to save the trees going to start?
I think the issue is pretty clear cut.
What's the zip for Harper's Ferry?

Uncle Tom's Sawmill

The whine of the saw
Rips the heart.

We'll all die if we can't have
Old growth trees to cut
Slaves to drive
Our own way.

Slow Down, Columbia Slow Down

With no apologies to Woody Guthrie, much less Arlo

There are still 23 miles of free flowing
Columbia River water in the state of Washington.
This ridiculous governmental oversight
Should be corrected immediately.

Woody Guthrie, on the government payroll,
Cranked out 30 songs in 30 days,
A fast writer on a slow river,
One Goddamned Dam after another.

Through this chain of lakes locked together,
The ghosts of anadromous salmon barge on regardless,
To seaports like Lewiston, Idaho,
Over the crest of the dioxin waves.

Mussolini Jones

I nurse a fetish to read from balconies.
To restore the indoor plumbing of Pompeii
Complete with a lead pipe cinch.
I'll embrace the bogus support of Ezra Pound.
Somebody has to make the little magazines publish on time.

I can probably pass on feeling my body
Dragged headless through the streets of Rome,
Tied behind Lina Wertmüller's jeep.

With .93 [point ninety-three] governments per year
Since WWII, Italy is an ancient satire on continuity,
That did not begin with Guiseppe Garibaldi.

If you can get great movies, great cars, great art, great shoes,
Great food, (ice cream was invented in *Firenze* Florence)
Without it, what is government good for?
Wertmüller, Ferrari, fettucine, Dante, Michelangelo,
Famolare, Lamborghini, Fellini, De Medici, etceteras.

Modus Operandum

I began composing *Nature Lovers* during the late summer of 1989 in order to have some new poems to read for what turned out to be a two state, five gigs in six days tour of Utah and Idaho. It is the first sustained poetry I wrote under the influence of both Neuro Linguistic Programming, at which I have since become a Master Practitioner, and my investigation of the micro structure of cognition. I had been reading *The Foundations of Neural Computing* and *Parallel Distributed Processing*.

Nature Lovers then, both in concept and diction, enabled me to take the poem farther into the response nodes of the receiving audience than I'd been before. This amazing process stimulated me to create in short order, an amount of poetry equivalent to the poetry of the previous decade, published in *A Rite to the Body* and *The Dictatorship of the Environment*. I go way back with writers who identify themselves with nature: Wordsworth, for the mystifying and mystical unity to be found there; Menzu, (Mencius) for his insistence that the entire state has to operate in obeisance to natural law; and Lucretius, who said poets should never lose the power to irritate.

I was paying dues literally during this period to half the famous environmental organizations on the planet including Greenpeace, The Nature Conservancy, The Audubon Society, The World Wildlife Fund, Earth First!, The Sierra Club et al and was diligently reading their publications. This reading put me at least part way up to speed on the major issues of the time.

The poems themselves insisted that I shed my own well protected innocence and naiveté as we went along and I came reluctantly to the conclusion that I was dealing with an oxymoron. There are no "nature lovers" worthy of the name, unless of course we consider the Sierra Clubbers and their annual grizzly bear feast where the lucky winner motors to Yellowstone and flings him or herself into the bear's mouth, grateful to be eaten alive. In the middle of the composition I came across and read *The End of Nature* by Bill McKibben and found the object of our "love" itself eroding rapidly away.

In my notes for "The Henry David Thoreau Volunteer Army" section, I alleged that I was trying to create some new real estate, or a real fighting force for some sacred earth. Some of these people were drafted—did not volunteer—and may feel like they are in a forced march to a different drummer—mine. In one way or another, I know something incriminating about them all. "Did you do my laundry? How can I be civilly disobedient without clean underwear, *Ma*?"

The strident qualities of this didacticism are deliberate and since they will affect different people in different ways, some people may prefer them in small doses. I looked for ever higher gears and a way to sustain breathing in the consistently rarefying atmosphere of despair. My search for appropriately heavy metaphors led me to titles such as "Uncle Tom's Sawmill" and "The Wooden Heart of John Brown." Civil War metaphors, like the transcontinental train the war was partially fought over, carry a lot of freight. It was during a discussion and defense of such alarmist provocateuring that I blurted out, "Shit, the South *won* the Civil War."

The poems were dampered off indefinitely as I escaped my own conclusions through the trap door of political and economic geography, writing *The Chill at Appomattox*, later to be published as its subtitle, *How the South Finally Won the Civil War*, and with the addition of a further subtitle, *And Controls the Political Future of the United States*. We and the nature from which we are irreconcilably separated will survive to the exact degree we are able to extinguish the Southern domination of American Political life.

Prior to my curing myself of paranoid schizophrenia, commencing in 1969 and continuing for two decades, I entertained the simple delusion that it would only take a little self sacrifice and restraint for human life to survive on earth, a perfectly crazy idea. Little did I realize then that I was not normal and the survivalist organizing principle of that illness prevented me from noticing that the vast majority of people are organized on the pleasure principle, not the survival principle. I pass for normal now and our well intended and self serving delusions regarding the natural world won't make them come true.

Language separated people from nature and made their case one of cultural history, a unique, wholly owned subsidiary of natural history. Wordsworth, in his "Ode: On the Intimations of Immortality From Recollections of Early Childhood," the greatest poem in English, makes the point that the separation is complete and irreversible: "Nothing can bring back that hour." People separated themselves from nature and there is no way back. In our struggle through the ice ages creating syntax upon which to hang our grammar, we grew progressively more weary of being eaten alive. It is not permitted now, except in rare cases. Once, when we were part of nature, it was the norm. We think we love nature but nature doesn't love us back.

Pleasure Boat Studio books:

Michael Blumenthal, *When History Enters the House: Essays from Central Europe,* ISBN 0-9651413-2-2 USA $15 248 pp nonfiction
Frances Driscoll, *The Rape Poems*
ISBN 0-9651413-1-4 USA $12.95 88 pp Poetry
Edward Harkness, *Saying the Necessary,* ISBN 0-9651413-7-3
(hardbound $22) ISBN 0-9651413-9-X (paper $14) USA poetry
William Slaughter, *The Politics of My Heart*
ISBN 0-9651413-0-6 USA $12.95 96 pp Poetry
Tung Nien, *Setting Out: The Education of Li-li,* Translated from Chinese
by **Mike O'Connor,** ISBN 0-9651413-3-0 USA $15 160 pp fiction
Irving Warner, *In Memory of Hawks, & Other Stories from Alaska*
ISBN 0-9651413-4-9 USA $15 210 pp fiction

Chapbook Series:

Andrew Schelling, *The Handful of Seeds: Three and a Half Essays*
ISBN 0-9651413-5-7 USA $7 36 pages nonfiction
Michael Daley, *Original Sin*
ISBN 0-9651413-6-5 USA $8 36 pages poetry

Forthcoming Pleasure Boat Studio books:

Richard Cohen, *Pronoun Music*
ISBN 1-929355-03-1 $16 fiction
Ken Harvey, *If You Were with Me Everything Would Be All Right*
ISBN 1-929355-02-5 $16 fiction
Al Kessler, *The 8th Day of the Week*
ISBN 1-929355-00-9 $16 fiction
Charles Potts, *Nature Lovers*
ISBN 1-929355-04-1 $10 poetry
Kate Reavey, *Too Small to Hold You*
ISBN 1-92935-05-x $8 poetry
Edwin Weihe, *Another Life & Other Stories*
ISBN 1-929355-01-7 $16 fiction

Pleasure Boat Studio Books from other presses (in limited editions):

Empty Bowl Press

Jody Aliesan, *Desire*, ISBN 0-912887-11-7 $7   poetry
Michael Daley, *The Straits*, ISBN 0-912887-04-4 $5   poetry
Michael Daley, editor, *In Our Hearts and Minds: The Northwest and Central America*, ISBN 0-912887-18-4 $10   poetry and prose
Susan Goldwitz, *Dreams of the Hand*, ISBN 0-912887-12-5 $8 poetry
Mike O'Connor, *The Basin: Poems from a Chinese Province*
ISBN 0-912887-20-6 $10 Poetry (paper or hardbound available)
Mike O'Connor, *Rainshadow*, No ISBN $10   poetry
Red Pine, *P'u Ming's Oxherding Tales*
No ISBN $7   Translations from Chinese with Illustrations   fiction
Red Pine, *The Mountain Poems of Stonehouse*
No ISBN $8   Translations from the Chinese   poetry
Mary Lou Sanelli, *Lineage*, No ISBN $7 poetry
William Slaughter, *Untold Stories*
ISBN 1-912887-24-9 $10   poetry (paper or hardbound available)

Broken Moon Press

Tim McNulty, *In Blue Mountain Dusk*
ISBN 0-9651413-8-1 $12.95   poetry

Pleasure Boat Studio   Tel-Fax 1-888-810-5308
8630 NE Wardwell Road   Email: pleasboat@aol.com
Bainbridge Island, WA 98110   URL: http://www.pbstudio.com

Pleasure Boat Studio books are also distributed by:

Small Press Distribution: Tel 800-869-7553--Fax 510-524-0852
Baker & Taylor: 800-775-1100--Fax 800-775-7480
Koen Pacific: 206-575-7544--Fax 206-575-7444
Partners/West: 425-227-8486--Fax 425-204-2448
Brodart: 800-233-8467--Fax 800-999-6799
Ingram: 800-937-800--Fax 800-876-0186